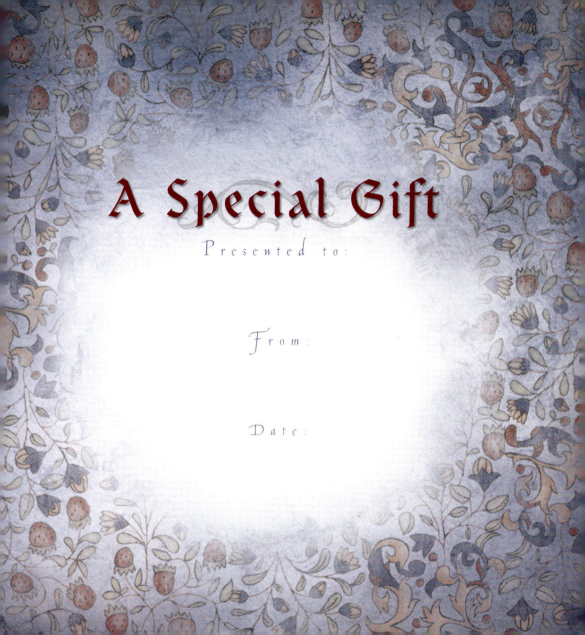

A Special Gift

Presented to:

From:

Date:

BLESSINGS OF HOPE
FROM THE LETTERS OF PAUL
A Title in the Illuminated Treasures Series

Published by Multnomah Gifts™, a division of Multnomah Publishers, Inc.
© 2002 by The Forest Hills Group
International Standard Book Number 1-59052-015-7

Written by Matthew A. Price
Designed by Anderson Thomas Design

Scripture quotations are from:
The Holy Bible, New International Version ©1973, 1978, 1984
by International Bible Society, used
by permission of Zondervan Publishing House. All rights reserved.

Multnomah is a trademark of Multnomah Publishers, Inc., and is
registered in the U.S. Patent and Trademark Office.
The colophon is a trademark of Multnomah Publishers, Inc.

Printed in China

For information:
Multnomah Publishers, Inc.
Post Office Box 1720
Sisters, Oregon 97759

BLESSINGS OF

HOPE

FROM THE

Letters of Paul

Illuminated
Treasures

DISCOVERING THE LIGHT
OF GOD'S WORD

Multnomah Gifts
Multnomah Publishers · Sisters, Oregon

Today, thankfully, the Bible is readily and affordably available to all who seek a daily relationship with Christ. Yet handy accessibility can also produce inattention to and underappreciation of the majesty and perfection of God's holy Word. ✺ Thus *Illuminated Treasures* is not simply a modern salute to the timeless tradition of artistically rendering Scripture. Its purpose ~ with images, design, and devotional text ~ is to draw you into the message of each verse and to bring you into a fuller awareness of how the Bible can apply to each situation, every circumstance, and all aspects of your life. ✺ May God richly bless you as you meditate on His Word and reflect on His perfect will for your life. ▨

MATTHEW A. PRICE, *Winter 2001*

A HISTORY OF ILLUMINATED TEXTS

Imagine for a moment that the singular task you have chosen for the rest of your life is to hand copy the Bible, hymnals, or prayer books. Now imagine that your tools consist only of the trimmed flight feathers of a goose, a penknife, sable hairs, sand, and small sticks. Your inks are a combination of ground lapis lazuli, molten sulfur, corrosion from copper plates, and carbon black. Your parchment has taken weeks to produce as farmers have dried the hides of dozens of newborn calves through a careful, multistep process. *F*inally you can begin inscribing the text ~ only you will not use the relatively easy method of carefully writing each word in clear, legible text. Instead you will painstakingly render each letter in calligraphic script, etch intricate designs around the borders, and draw elaborate pictures representing scenes and themes from the passages on the page. *I*f this process seems unimaginable, then you can appreciate the world we live in, where books, magazines, and other reading materials are as common and plentiful as grass in a meadow. You can also see why before the advent of movable type, only institutions like the church and the very wealthy could afford to own a single book ~ or an illuminated manuscript as they are appropriately known. ❀ So you may be wondering, who would dedicate painful, solitary hours each day, each week, each month, for years on end to the task of producing a work that would only be appreciated by a select few? And what would inspire them to make this personal sacrifice? ❀

While some illuminated manuscripts were the products of paid artisans and craftsmen, the majority of the books produced prior to the thirteenth century were the handiwork of anonymous monks, canons, and nuns. For these dedicated scribes, remuneration and satisfaction came not from material gain or personal glory. Rather they labored in joyful service to their Lord. They held firm to the conviction that the Word of God, and the prayers and hymns written to praise Him, should be treated in such a manner that would highlight and celebrate the infinite importance of the text and effectively direct the reader's attention to the substance of key words and passages. ▨

Be still, my soul ~ thy God doth undertake
To guide the future, as He has the past;
Thy hope, thy confidence let nothing shake ~
All now mysterious shall be bright at last.
Be still, my soul ~ the waves and winds shall know
His voice who ruled them while He dwelt below.

KATHARINA VON SCHLEGEL
"Be Still, My Soul"

In all these things we are more than conquerors through him who loved us. For I am convinced that neither death nor life, neither angels nor demons, neither the present nor the future, nor any powers, neither height nor depth, nor anything else in all creation, will be able to separate us from the love of God that is in Christ Jesus our Lord.

ROMANS 8:37~39

For God is not
a God of disorder
but of peace.

1 CORINTHIANS 14:33

Throughout Scripture we are given examples of God's infallible perfection. He is the essence of all that is true and holy and pure. If you are going through a situation that is confusing and uncertain, turn to Him in earnest prayer and immerse yourself in His Word. Place your hope solely in His hands, and you will find lasting peace and comfort.

God is the essence of all that is perfect and ordered. When life seems hopeless, remember that God loves you, that He will never deceive you, and that He has a flawless plan for your life. Trials will come, but remember that the God who has been faithful in the past will be faithful today to bring peace to your life.

On him we have set our hope that he will continue to deliver us....

2 Corinthians 1:10

And when we arrive at the haven of rest,

We shall hear the glad words, "Come up hither, you blest,

Here are regions of light, here are mansions of bliss."

Oh, who would not climb such a ladder as this?

"JACOB'S LADDER"
Anonymous Folk Hymn

Therefore you do not lack any spiritual gift as you eagerly wait for our Lord Jesus Christ to be revealed. He will keep you strong to the end, so that you will be blameless on the day of our Lord Jesus Christ.

1 CORINTHIANS 1:7~8

The fruit of
the Spirit is

The fruit of the

love, joy, peace,
patience, kind-
ness, goodness,
faithfulness,
gentleness and
self-control.

GALATIANS 5:22~23

Spirit is love

O God, our Heavenly Father, in You is
found all hope of glory. In You is the sole
promise of the bright riches of eternity ~ an
eternity where we will experience perfect love,
perfect joy, and perfect peace. We praise You
for Your steadfast faithfulness. We worship
You for Your abundant mercy. We thank You
for creating us in Your image. And we pray
that You will fill us with the holiness of Your
Spirit. In the name of Your Son, our Savior,
Jesus Christ we pray, amen.

Sometimes the best advice is the most difficult to accept. When circumstances seem hopeless and sleepless nights are followed by weary days, it's difficult to embrace the words of Paul ~ to cast aside anxiety and rejoice in the Lord. Yet God's love for you has no boundaries. He hears the silent petitions of your heart and sees the tears you've shed. His desire is for you to draw closer to Him and to experience the fullness of His merciful kindness and transcending peace. Whether it's the loss of a job, concern for a child's welfare, or another situation that seems entirely beyond your control, God is able to fill you with the same warm assurance He gave to Paul and countless Christians since. Turn to Him today. He wants to listen and He will surely respond.

Rejoice in the Lord always.... Do not be anxious about anything, but in everything, by prayer and petition, with thanksgiving, present your requests to God. And the peace of God, which transcends all understanding, will guard your hearts and your minds in Christ Jesus.

PHILIPPIANS 4:4, 6~7

He sends the sunshine and the rain,
He sends the harvest's golden grain;
Sunshine and rain, harvest of grain,
He's my friend.

WILL L. THOMPSON
"Jesus Is All the World to Me"

If ever there was a reason to have hope for the future, it is to know that the
Creator of the universe cared enough to die for you, to conquer death for you,
and to stand before God on your behalf. He is the one perfect and true friend
you have. And what a friend He is!

But when the kindness and love of God our Savior appeared, he saved us, not because of righteous things we had done, but because of his mercy.... So that, having been justified by his grace, we might become heirs having the hope of eternal life.

TITUS 3:4~5, 7

*Praise be to the God and Father
of our Lord Jesus Christ,
the Father of compassion and
the God of all comfort,
who comforts us in all our troubles,
so that we can comfort those
in any trouble with the comfort we
ourselves have received from God.*

2 CORINTHIANS 1:3~4

So often the most loving and compassionate Christians are those who have experienced great difficulties and trials in their lives. Despite their circumstances or the challenges they have overcome, they radiate the peace and joy of the Lord. These blessed individuals understand fully the great spiritual paradox that when comfort is given to others, greater comfort is received in return. When, in the name of Christ, we share the wisdom we've gained from the challenges we've faced, our own burdens are miraculously eased.

Therefore, since we have been justified through faith, we have peace with God through our Lord Jesus Christ.... And we rejoice in the hope of the glory of God.

ROMANS 5:1~2

Jesus is more ready to pardon than you are to sin. He is more
willing to supply your wants than you are to confess them.
Never tolerate low thoughts of Him. You may study, look, and
meditate, but Jesus is a greater Savior than you think Him to be
when your thoughts are at their highest.

CHARLES HADDON SPURGEON

And God is able to make all grace abound to you, so that in all things at all times, having all that you need, you will abound in every good work.

2 CORINTHIANS 9:8

And now these three remain: faith, hope and love. But the greatest of these is love.

1 CORINTHIANS 13:13

Remember that without faith there can be no hope and that hope produces a spirit of assurance and confidence that opens the heart to the peace and joy that only love for others can bring.

*All who call on God in true faith, earnestly from the heart,
will certainly be heard, and will receive what they have asked
and desired, although not in the hour or in the measure,
or the very thing which they ask; yet they will obtain something
greater and more glorious than they had dared to ask.*

MARTIN LUTHER

We have this hope as an anchor for the soul, firm and secure.

HEBREWS 6:19

Be joyful always; pray continually; give thanks in all circumstances,

pray continually

for this is God's will for you in Christ Jesus.

1 Thessalonians 5:16~18

At some point in life all people experience a crisis over which they have little or no control: physical illness, depression, a broken marriage, the death of a child, the loss of a job. The Bible has a remedy for conquering sorrow and achieving victory over despair: "Be joyful always; pray continually; give thanks in all circumstances." It may sound like a cliché or too good to be true, but it always works because God is faithful to those who trust in Him.

Prayer opens the heart to God, and it is the means by which the soul, though empty, is filled by God.

JOHN BUNYAN

Be joyful in hope, patient in affliction, faithful in prayer.

ROMANS 12:12

When speaking about prayer, many pastors and Christian writers note that it is difficult, if not impossible, to have a relationship with someone to whom you never speak. To truly have a meaningful, committed relationship with Jesus Christ, you must have a regular, daily conversation with Him. Nothing ~ absolutely nothing ~ will fill you with hope and joy like closing your eyes, quieting your mind, and filling your heart with the presence of Christ through prayer.

For our light and momentary troubles are achieving for us an eternal glory that far outweighs them all.

2 Corinthians 4:17

The life of every
Christian ~ from the
beginning to the end,
through each obstacle and
challenge ~ is a process of
refinement, guided by the
hand of God, that makes
us stronger and more
resilient while at the same
time reinforcing our
reliance on the infinite
wisdom of the Holy Spirit
and providing hope
for eternity.

For in this hope we were saved. But hope that is seen is no hope at all.... And we know that in all things *God works for* God works for the good of those who love him, who have been called according to his purpose.

ROMANS 8:24, 28

My hope is built on nothing less,
Than Jesus' blood and righteousness.
I dare not trust the sweetest frame,
But wholly lean on Jesus' name.

EDWARD MOTE
"The Solid Rock"

the good

The whole world is looking for more power, more riches, more enlightenment. From great Western nations to third world states, from rulers to average citizens, everyone wants to experience in abundance the tarnished crown of temporal distinction. Yet true glory can only come by humbling ourselves to embrace the cross upon which our precious Savior gave His life to save both the great and small. Only then can a person fully encounter the hope to which God has called each of us and the "great power" for all who believe.

Be joyful in hope...

ROMANS 12:12

hope

And hope does not
disappoint us, because
God has poured out
his love into our hearts
by the Holy Spirit,
whom he has given us.

ROMANS 5:5

Hope is the one constant in the life of each Christian who has achieved great things for the Kingdom. From a parent's hope for a child to a missionary's hope for a nation, there is no other conviction like hope to make a believer rise up each day excited about the possibilities that lie ahead.

As true and deep and challenging as Paul's letters are, they are also filled with great love and compassion for those to whom he ministered ~ despite the fact that his own daily existence was marked by hardship, suffering, and danger. His joy came from the knowledge that Christ had saved him from the sins and strife of this world and that all his trials were nothing compared to the hope of glory that awaited him in heaven.

If you have any encouragement from being united with Christ, if any comfort from his love, if any fellowship with the Spirit, if any tenderness and compassion, then make my joy complete by being like~minded, having the same love, being one in spirit and purpose.

PHILIPPIANS 2:1~2

I pray also that the eyes of your heart may be enlightened in order that you may know the hope to which he has called you, the riches of his glorious inheritance in the saints, and his incomparably great power for us who believe.

EPHESIANS 1:18~19

May the God of hope fill you with all joy and peace as you trust in him, so that you may overflow with hope by the power of the Holy Spirit.

ROMANS 15:13

In times of affliction we commonly meet with the sweetest experiences of the love of God.

JOHN BUNYAN

May our Lord Jesus Christ himself and God our Father, who loved us and by his grace gave us eternal encouragement and good hope, encourage your hearts and strengthen you in every good deed and word.

2 THESSALONIANS 2:16~17